SCHIRMER'S LIBRARY
OF MUSICAL CLASSICS

Vol. 1960c

GEORGE FRIDERIC HANDEL

Concerto in B♭

Transcribed for Harp Solo
with an Original Cadenza

By Carlos Salzedo

G. SCHIRMER, Inc.

DISTRIBUTED BY
HAL•LEONARD®
CORPORATION
7777 W. BLUEMOUND RD. P.O. BOX 13819 MILWAUKEE, WI 53213

T0051120

PREFACE

Carlos Salzedo was born in Arcachon, France, on April 6, 1885, and died in Waterville, Maine, on August 17, 1961. He trained at the Conservatories of Bordeaux and Paris, studying composition, piano and harp. He emigrated to the United States and served under Toscanini as first harpist of the Metropolitan Opera orchestra. He continued to compose, mainly for the harp, and voice and chamber instruments, employing rhythmic complexities inspired by his Basque upbringing, and to transcribe the works of other composers. Salzedo was a well-known organizer of musical activities, a publisher and a proponent of contemporary music. In 1924 he formed the harp department at the Curtis Institute of Music where he taught for 38 years. He founded the Salzedo Harp Colony in Camden, Maine, which has educated generations of harp students since 1931. Instrument manufacturers adopted many of his proposals for modernizing the contours of the harp. In his books, principally in *Modern Study of the Harp*, published by Schirmer in 1921, he developed a revolutionary set of ideas and effects that have since become part of standard harp technique. Leopold Stokowski referred to him as "the first and only composer in the world who knew how to compose for the harp according to its true nature."

Handel wrote the Concerto in B♭ to illustrate "the Power of Musick" in his 1736 oratorio *Alexander's Feast,* celebrating the patron saint of music, St. Cecilia. It follows the recitative concerning the Greek bard Timotheus:

> Timotheus plac'd on high,
> Amid the tuneful Quire,
> With flying fingers touch'd the Lyre:
> The trembling Notes ascend the Sky,
> And heav'nly Joys inspire.

During the Second World War, Eugene Ormandy engaged Carlos Salzedo to perform this concerto with the Philadelphia Orchestra. Salzedo was unable to consult original manuscripts in Europe and had to rely on extant versions of the concerto for the performance. He wrote an extended cadenza for inclusion between the last two movements.

—Lucile Lawrence

EXPLANATION OF HARPISTIC SYMBOLS — EXPLICATION DES SIGNES HARPISTIQUES

0 0
  0

Harmonies are written where they actually sound; they are produced on the string an octave lower.
Les sons harmoniques sont écrits en sons réels; ils sont produits sur la corde à l'octave basse de la note indiquée.

.

A dot above or under the fingering or at the end of the placing symbol (⌐⎯⎯⎯⎯⌐) means to leave after a note, that is, not to connect.
Un point au-dessus ou au-dessous d'un doigté ou à la fin du signe pour placer (⌐⎯⎯⎯⌐) veut dire de quitter après la note, c'est à dire, de ne pas placer.

to play very close to the sounding board: "Guitaric Sounds"
pour jouer tout près de la table d'harmonie: "Sons guitariques"

indicates a series of "Isolated Sounds" (fingering indicated)
indique une série de "Sons isolés" (doigté indiqué)

to muffle
pour étouffer

$\frac{1}{2}$ ⊕

to muffle lightly
pour étouffer légèrement

to play a passage in "Muffled Sounds"
pour jouer un passage en "Sons étouffés"

to muffle a specific string: "Individual muffling" (fingering indicated)
pour étouffer une corde spécifiée: "Étouffé individuel" (doigté indiqué)

to muffle a specified group of strings
pour étouffer un groupe spécifié de cordes

to muffle totally
pour étouffer totalement

L.V.

to let vibrate
pour laisser vibrer

Concerto in B♭

Transcribed for Harp Solo
or to be played with orchestral accompaniment*
with an original Cadenza by
Carlos Salzedo

George Frideric Handel
(1685 - 1759)

*In this edition the harp plays continuously, including the orchestral *tutti*.

1) On the 3rd count, muffle the E♭ (of the 2nd count) with the back of the 2nd finger. Same procedure on the 1st count of the following measure.

Au 3me temps, étouffer le Mi♭ (du 2me temps) avec le dos du 2me doigt. De même, au 1er temps de la mesure suivante.

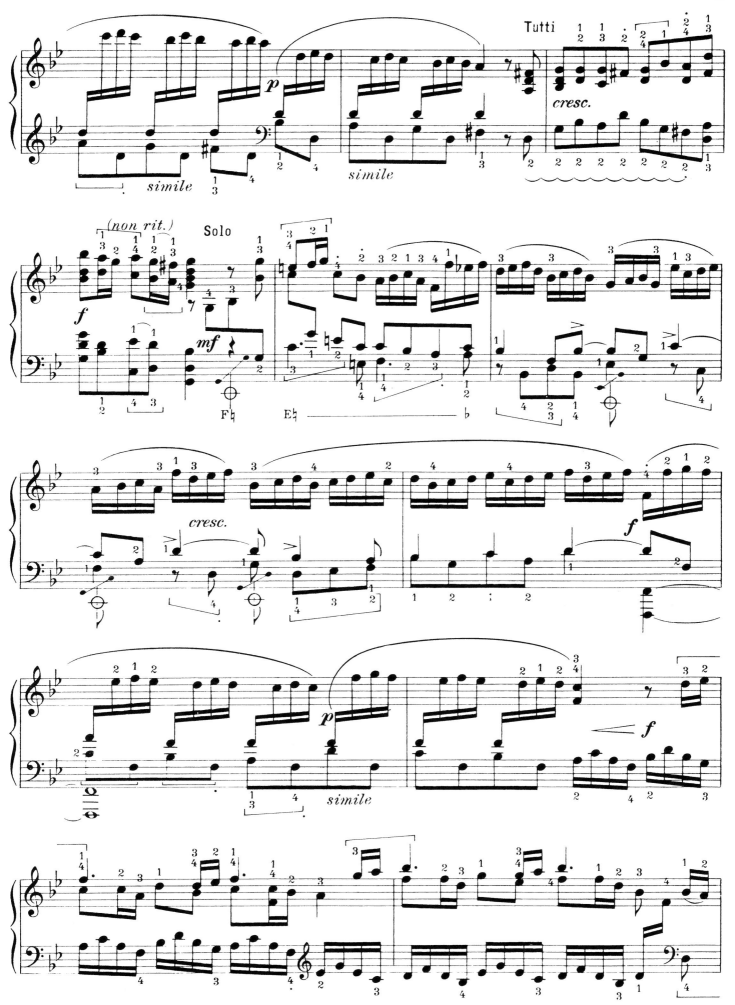

1) In order to eliminate the preceding octaves play the 1st octave in each measure hand open, and play other *octaves with fingers down.*
Afin d'éliminer les octaves précédentes, jouer la 1r octave de chaque mesure la main ouverte, et les autres octaves avec les doigts en bas.

2) Facility

Cadenza

Carlos Salzedo

1) On the 2nd count muffle the F♯ (of the 1st count) with the back of the 3rd finger.
Au 2eme temps ètouffez le Fa♯ (de 1re temps) avec le dos du 3me doigt.

Allegro moderato

Tutti